# Show Me REPTILES

## My First Picture Encyclopedia

by Megan Cooley Peterson

Consultant:
Staff at Reptile Gardens
Rapid City, South Dakota

CAPSTONE PRESS
a capstone imprint

A+ Books are published by Capstone Press,
1710 Roe Crest Drive, North Mankato, Minnesota 56003.
www.capstonepub.com

*Library of Congress Cataloging-in-Publication Data*
Peterson, Megan Cooley.
 Show me reptiles : my first picture encyclopedia / by Megan Cooley Peterson.
   p. cm. — (A+ books. My first picture encyclopedias)
 Summary: "Defines through text and photos core terms related to reptiles"—Provided
   by publisher.
 ISBN 978-1-4296-8571-9 (library binding)
 ISBN 978-1-62065-197-1 (ebook PDF)
 1. Reptiles—Juvenile literature. 2. Picture books for children.  I. Title.
 QL644.2.P46 2013
 597.9—dc23              2012007353

**Editorial Credits**

Kristen Mohn, editor; Tracy Davies McCabe, designer; Svetlana Zhurkin, media researcher; Laura Manthe, production specialist

**Photo Credits**

Alamy: David Boag, 11 (bottom left), Françoise Emily, 29 (top right); AP Photo: Penn State University/Blair Hedge, 29 (top left); Corbis: Visuals Unlimited/Jim Merli, 27 (top left); Corel, 31 (middle right and left, and bottom); Dreamstime: Au_yeung225, 30 (top), Brendan Van Son, 19 (bottom), Casey Bishop, 14 (top), Davidschonborn, 25 (bottom right), Geens, 10 (bottom right), Hadot, 10 (middle right), Karin Van Ijzendoorn, 23 (middle left), Mgkuijpers, 17 (middle), 26 (top right), Morten Elm, 21 (bottom left), Mpalis, 27 (top right), Nathalie Speliers Ufermann, 23 (top), Omar Ariff Kamarul Ariffin, 8 (top right), Robert Bayer, 28 (bottom left), Snezana Skundric, 14 (bottom), Stephen Noakes, 18 (bottom), Tjkphotography, 11 (top right); Getty Images: Photo Researchers, 31 (top), Tom McHugh, 25 (middle); iStockphotos: Klaas Lingbeek van Kranen, 10–11 (back), Richard Lathulerie, 12 (bottom), Todd Winner, 24 (bottom left); National Geographic Stock: George Grall, 10 (middle left), Joel Sartore, 29 (bottom); Nature Picture Library: Tony Phelps, 11 (top left and middle); Newscom: AFP/S. Blair Hedges, 28 (right), Danita Delimont Photography/Pete Oxford, 21 (top left), Getty Images/AFP/Yuri Cortez, 11 (bottom right), Photoshot/Evolve/Stephen Dalton, 21 (top right and middle), 26 (bottom); Shutterstock: Aleksander Bolbot, 6 (bottom back), Alex Edmonds, 24 (right), Alexander Cherednichenko, 6 (bottom), amadorgs (iguana), cover, Anan Kaewkhammul, 12 (top), Anna Utekhina, 4 (bottom left), Arkady (cactus), cover, Audrey Snider-Bell, 8 (middle), Cameramannz, 7 (middle left), Cathy Keifer, 13 (bottom right), 22 (top and bottom right), choikh, 4 (top right), Chris Driscoll, 20 (top), Chuck Rausin, 13 (top left), Daniel Alvarez, 27 (middle left), David Persson, 28 (top), DenisNata, 16 (bottom left), Dr. Morley Read, 24 (top), EcoPrint, 25 (top), Elnur (torn paper), cover, 1, Eric Isselée, cover (turtle and chameleon), back cover (right), 1, 4 (top left), 5 (middle, bottom left and middle), 7 (top left, middle right, and bottom right), 13 (top right and bottom left), 15 (top), 17 (top), 20 (bottom left and right), 23 (bottom), 27 (middle right and bottom), erllre74, 22 (bottom left), Evok20, 5 (top right), fivespots, cover (python), back cover (left), 8 (bottom left and right). 9 (top and bottom), 16 (top), Heiko Kiera, 18 (top), James A. Dawson, 19 (middle left), Karen Givens, 6 (top right), Kjersti Joergensen, 21 (bottom right), liubomir, 16 (middle), Mammut Vision, 6 (top left), mashe, 7 (bottom left), Matt Jeppson, 15 (middle left), Norman Bateman, 19 (middle right), objectsforall, 7 (top right), Olena Istomina (lizards), cover and throughout, Pan Xunbin, 4 (bottom right), 9 (middle left), Petra B. Zaugg, 8 (top left), Radoslaw Lecyk, 25 (bottom left), Robynrg, 19 (top), Rufous (hatching crocodile), cover, Ryan M. Bolton (coral snake), 27, s_oleg, 5 (top left), Sasilssolutions, 15 (bottom), Sergey Uryadnikov, 29 (middle), sippakorn, 15 (middle right), Steffen Foerster Photography, 30 (bottom), Timothy Craig Lubcke, 23 (middle right), Trent Townsend, 17 (bottom), WitR, 5 (bottom right), xpixel, 9 (middle right); Wikipedia: Zylornian, 9 (back), 26 (top left)

**Note to Parents, Teachers, and Librarians**

My First Picture Encyclopedias provide an early introduction to reference materials for young children. These accessible, visual encyclopedias support literacy development by building subject-specific vocabularies and research skills. Stimulating format, inviting content, and phonetic aids assist and encourage young readers.

Printed in the United States of America in North Mankato, Minnesota.
042012    006682CGF12

# Table of Contents

# Reptiles in the Animal Kingdom

Reptiles belong to the animal kingdom, a group that includes all animals. Here are some of the main groups in the animal kingdom.

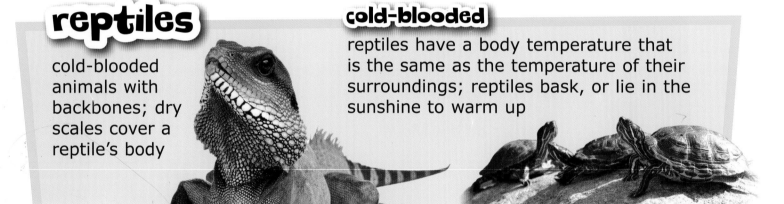

## reptiles

cold-blooded animals with backbones; dry scales cover a reptile's body

## cold-blooded

reptiles have a body temperature that is the same as the temperature of their surroundings; reptiles bask, or lie in the sunshine to warm up

## mammals

(MAM-uhls)—warm-blooded animals that have backbones and hair or fur instead of scales; female mammals feed milk to their young

## insects

small animals with hard outer shells, six legs, three body sections, and two antennae; most insects have wings

## birds

warm-blooded animals that have feathers and wings and can lay eggs

## fish

cold-blooded animals that live in water and have scales, fins, and gills

## amphibians

(am-FI-bee-uhns) cold-blooded animals with backbones and wet skin

# Amphibians Aren't Reptiles

**larva**

(LAR-vuh)—most amphibians are born as larvae that look very different from adults; baby reptiles look like small adults

**egg**

amphibian eggs are soft; reptiles lay hard or leathery eggs

amphibians have smooth, wet skin while reptiles have dry, scaly skin; amphibians can also breathe through their skin

**skin**

# Meet the Reptiles

From creeping crocodiles to slithering snakes, reptiles live almost everywhere on Earth. There are more than 8,000 kinds of reptiles, which scientists have divided into groups. Here are some of the most common groups.

## alligators and crocodiles

large reptiles that have strong jaws and sharp teeth used to kill other animals; alligators and crocodiles spend much of their time in the water

## Alligator or Crocodile?

**jaw**

alligators have U-shaped jaws while crocodiles have V-shaped jaws; an alligator's bottom teeth are not visible when its jaws are closed, but a crocodile's are

crocodile

# turtles and tortoises

reptiles that can pull their heads, legs, and tails into their hard shells for protection; turtles live in water and on land, but tortoises live only on land

# tuataras

(too-uh-TAR-uhs) lizardlike reptiles that live only in New Zealand; they sleep during the day and hunt at night

# geckos

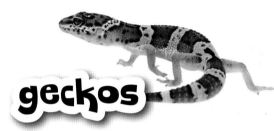

(GEK-ohs)—small, harmless lizards often found in houses in warm countries; geckos make squeaking and barking sounds

# chameleons

(kuh-MEEL-yuhns)—lizards that can change their skin color

# iguanas

(i-GWAH-nuhs)—lizards with four legs and long tails; green iguanas can grow to be more than 5 feet (1.5 meters) long

## colubrids

boomslang

(KAHL-yoo-brids) more than half of all snakes belong to the colubrid family; both deadly boomslangs and harmless garter snakes are colubrids

## cobras

(KOH-bruhs)—large, venomous snakes; some cobras spread their neck skin to look like a hood

## vipers

(VYE-purs)—a family of venomous snakes, such as rattlesnakes

## pythons

(PYE-thons)—large, powerful snakes that wrap themselves around prey and suffocate it; female pythons lay eggs

## boas

(BOH-uhs)—tropical snakes that kill their prey by wrapping around it and squeezing; female boas give birth to live young

## beaded lizards

large, slow-moving lizards found in Mexico, Guatemala, and the southwestern United States; a beaded lizard called the Gila (HEE-luh) monster is the only venomous lizard in the United States

## skinks

the largest lizard family; skinks are slow-moving and have small legs

## worm lizards

a kind of lizard that looks like a snake; these reptiles dig tunnels and live underground

## monitor lizards

lizards with long necks, short bodies, and strong tails

# From Egg to Adult

## life cycle

the series of changes that take place in a living thing, from birth to death; the life cycle for most reptiles begins with an egg

## life span

the number of years a certain animal usually lives; sand lizards can live for 12 years

## egg tooth

a sharp bump on top of a lizard's or snake's snout, used to cut out of an egg

## hatchling

a young reptile that has just come out of its egg

**nest** to build a nest, the female sand lizard digs a hole in sandy soil

**guard** to watch over and keep safe; unlike most reptiles, crocodiles guard their young

**egg layers** most reptiles lay eggs

**clutch** a group of eggs; the female sand lizard lays four to 14 eggs in the nest, covers them, and leaves

**hatch** to break out of an egg; after about two months, the young sand lizards hatch; they live on their own after hatching

**live birth** some snakes and lizards give live birth instead of laying eggs

# What Reptiles Look Like

Scaly skin. Long tails. Sharp teeth. Reptiles might look scary, but their body parts help them find food and stay safe.

## teeth

most reptiles have teeth; alligator and crocodile teeth are lost and replaced thousands of times!

## beak

the hard, pointed part of an animal's mouth; turtles have no teeth—they use their pointy beaks to cut food

## shell

a hard, outer covering that keeps turtles safe

## webbed feet

feet with wide flaps of skin between the toes; a turtle's webbed feet help it swim; tortoises live on land and do not have webbed feet

## fang

a long,
hollow tooth

## forked tongue

the moveable muscle in
the mouths of snakes,
beaded lizards, and monitor
lizards; the forked tongue is
used to collect smells

## snout

the long front part of a
reptile's face, including its
nose, mouth, and jaws

## dewlap

(DOO-lap)—the loose skin
that hangs under the chin
or neck of some reptiles

## claw

a hard curved nail
on the foot of some
reptiles used for
climbing, fighting,
and digging

## scale

one of the small,
hard plates that
covers a reptile's body

## sticky tongue

chameleons shoot
out their long, sticky
tongues to
catch insects

# Skin and Scales

A reptile's dry, scaly skin might look strange. But for reptiles, dry skin is good! It helps keep water inside their bodies. Take a closer look at the skin and scales of reptiles.

## keeled scales

scales that have ridges running down their centers

## clear scales

a snake doesn't have eyelids that move; instead, clear scales cover a snake's eyes

## keratin

(KAIR-uh-tin)—the hard material that makes up a reptile's scales; your fingernails are also made of keratin

## granular scales

(GRAN-yuh-luhr)—small, bumpy scales that don't overlap

## smooth scales

scales that have a regular or even surface, without roughness or bumps

## molt

to shed the outer layer of skin so new skin can grow; some lizards eat the dead skin they shed because nutrients in the skin help them grow

## armor

(AR-muhr)—bones, scales, or skin that some animals have on their bodies for protection; crocodiles have bony plates in their skin

# A Turtle's Shell

Can you imagine carrying your home on your back?
A turtle's shell protects its head, limbs, and body.
All turtles have shells, but they don't all look the same.

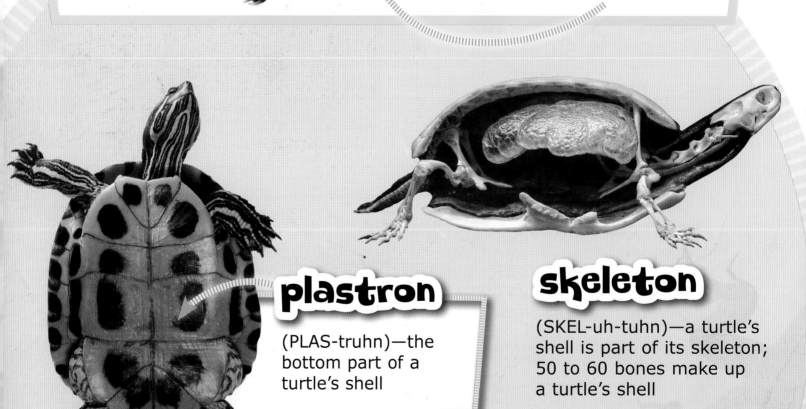

## carapace

(KAYR-uh-pace)
the top part of a
turtle's shell

## scute

(SKOOT)—one of
the large, hard
scales that covers
a turtle's shell

## plastron

(PLAS-truhn)—the
bottom part of a
turtle's shell

## skeleton

(SKEL-uh-tuhn)—a turtle's
shell is part of its skeleton;
50 to 60 bones make up
a turtle's shell

## exhale

(eks-HALE)—turtles push the air out of their lungs to make room for their heads and legs inside their shells

## ring

as turtles grow, their scutes make rings on their shells; scientists count the rings to tell how old a turtle is

## straight-neck turtles

to stay safe, some turtles can pull their heads and legs completely into their shells

## side-neck turtles

not all turtles can pull their heads and legs into their shells; a side-neck turtle turns its head sideways and tucks it against its shell

## soft shell

some turtle shells are covered with leathery skin instead of scutes

# What's for Dinner?

Most reptiles eat other animals, but some snack on plants. Take a look at what's on a reptile's menu.

## prey

(PRAY)—an animal hunted by another animal for food; many reptiles hunt insects, mammals, birds, or fish

## squeeze

boas and pythons squeeze prey to death before eating it; some boas and pythons can live for a year on a single meal

## carnivore

(KAHR-nuh-vor)—an animal that eats only meat; most reptiles are carnivores; all crocodiles and snakes eat only meat

## predator

(PRED-uh-tur)
an animal that
hunts other animals
for food; most reptiles
are predators

## swallow

snakes don't
chew their food;
they swallow
it whole

## omnivore

(OM-nuh-vor)—an animal
that eats both plants and
animals; sea turtles eat
plants, fish, and crabs

## herbivore

(HUR-buh-vor)—an animal
that eats only plants;
some lizards and turtles
are herbivores

## algae

(AL-jee)—small plants without
roots or stems that grow in
water; marine iguanas are the
only lizards that eat algae

# Reptiles on the Move

They run! They swim! They fly through the air!
Watch out for reptiles on the move.

## flipper

one of the broad, flat limbs of a sea creature; flippers push sea turtles through the ocean

## migrate

(MYE-grate)—to move from one place to another when seasons change in order to find food or to lay eggs; female sea turtles return to the beaches where they were born to lay their eggs

## grip

geckos have sticky toes that grip almost any surface; they can even hang upside down

## slither

snakes move muscles in their bodies to slide along the ground

## dive

marine iguanas swish their tails from side to side to dive for algae

## glide

flying dragons glide between rain forest trees by spreading out folds of skin on the sides of their bodies; they can glide 200 feet (61 meters) in a single leap

## sprint

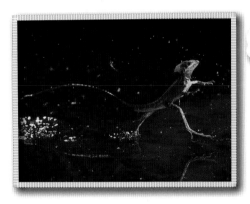

a short, fast run; basilisks run on their back legs; folds of skin along the sides of their toes help them dart across water

# Slow and Fast

### Galàpagos tortoise

(guh-LOP-uh-guhs)—tortoises are one of the slowest reptiles; the average person walks 17 times faster than the Galàpagos tortoise

the spiny-tailed iguana is the fastest reptile on land; it runs at speeds of 22 miles per hour (35 kilometers per hour)

### spiny-tailed iguana

# Reptile Senses

Do you spot a resting reptile? Reptiles keep busy even when they're not moving. They use their senses to escape danger and find their next meal.

## slit pupil

(PYOO-puhl)—a pupil is the dark center of a reptile's eye that lets in light; reptiles that are active at night have slit pupils

## taste bud

one of the small organs on the top of the tongue that tells animals and people what things taste like; lizards and crocodiles have taste buds, but snakes do not

## round pupil

reptiles that are active during the day, such as iguanas, have round pupils

## eye movement

chameleons can move each eye on its own; they can look at two different objects at the same time

# third eye

lizards and tuataras have a "third eye" on the tops of their heads that is covered with scales; although the third eye cannot see, it may help lizards sense what time of day it is

# sensory pit

(SEN-suh-ree)—alligators and crocodiles have small, black speckles on their jaws called sensory pits; these pits help them feel movement in the water made by their prey

# Jacobson's organ

an organ on the roof of the mouth of snakes and lizards; the tongue picks up scents and carries them to the Jacobson's organ

# heat pit

pythons, boas, and pit vipers use pits on their faces to feel the heat from their prey; the heat tells snakes when prey is near

python

# vibration

(vye-BRAY-shuhn)—a fast movement back and forth; snakes don't "hear" with ears—they feel vibrations that move through the ground

# Home Sweet Home

From deserts to oceans, reptiles live in almost every habitat on Earth. Some hang out in the treetops. Others burrow underground. Reptiles make their homes on every continent except Antarctica.

## rain forest

a thick area of trees where rain falls almost every day; large numbers of snakes and lizards live in rain forests

## ocean

(OH-shuhn)—a large body of salt water; the ocean is home to sea turtles, sea snakes, and marine iguanas

## adaptation

(a-dap-TAY-shuhn)—a change a living thing goes through over time to better fit in with its environment; snakes that live in trees are long and thin in order to climb

## desert

(DEH-zuhrt)—a dry area that gets little rain; many deserts are hot and sandy; lizards are the most common type of reptile found in deserts

## burrow

a tunnel or hole in the ground made or used by an animal; desert reptiles enter their burrows to escape the heat

## hibernate

(HYE-bur-nate)—to spend the winter in a deep sleep; reptiles that live in colder places hibernate

## freshwater

water that does not contain salt; turtles, crocodiles, and snakes live in rivers, streams, ponds, and lakes

## nocturnal

(nok-TUR-nuhl)—active at night; desert and rain forest geckos escape the heat by resting during the day

# Sneaky Survivors

Lizards that spit blood. Snakes that play dead. Reptiles have found lots of sneaky ways to survive. They hide from enemies but also use defenses to stay safe.

## blood

horned lizards squirt blood from their eyes to scare away predators

## startle

(STAR-tuhl)—to surprise or frighten; blue-tongued skinks stick out their brightly colored tongues and hiss to scare away hungry birds and other animals

## venom

(VEN-uhm)—a poison that some animals make; cobras, vipers, komodo dragons, Mexican beaded lizards, and Gila monsters kill their prey with venom

## rattle

venomous rattlesnakes have hollow scales at the ends of their tails; they shake them to make a warning sound

## play dead

some reptiles, such as hognose snakes and chameleons, roll over and play dead if threatened; some predators won't eat animals they think are dead

## drop tail

some lizards drop their tails to escape enemies; new tails slowly grow

## camouflage

(KA-muh-flahzh)—coloring that makes animals look like their surroundings; many snakes and lizards that live in trees are green to help them blend in

## mimicry

**milk snake**

**coral snake**

(MIM-ih-kree)—the act of looking like something or someone else; the milksnake has brightly colored skin that looks like the deadly coral snake; predators pass up the milksnake and look for something safer to eat

## puffy throat

frilled lizards fan out the skin around their throats to scare off other animals

# Reptile Record Holders

Large reptiles are easy to spot. Others are so small, you might miss them! Take a peek at these reptile record holders.

## green anaconda

(an-uh-KAHN-duh)—one of the world's longest snakes, the green anaconda, can grow more than 30 feet (9 meters) long; its size helps it kill large animals such as deer

## dwarf gecko

(DWORF)—at just 0.6 inches (1.5 centimeters) long, the dwarf gecko is the world's smallest lizard and reptile; it hides under leaves on rain forest floors

## saltwater crocodile

the largest living reptile hides its 2,220-pound (1,007-kilogram) body below the water's surface; it bursts out of the water to grab large prey like kangaroos

# Barbados thread snake

(bar-BAY-dohs)—not all snakes are big; the world's shortest snake is only about 4 inches (10 cm) long

# leatherback turtle

the largest turtle grows to 6 feet (1.8 m) long; it weighs about 2,000 pounds (907 kg), which is as heavy as a small car

# komodo dragon

(kuh-MOH-doh)—the komodo dragon is the world's largest lizard; it weighs about 300 pounds (136 kg) and grows up to 10 feet (3 m) long

# speckled padloper

(SPEK-uhld PAD-loh-puhr) the smallest turtle grows up to 4 inches (10 cm) long; its rocklike shell blends in with its rocky habitat

# Ancient Reptiles

Dinosaurs were relatives of reptiles and lived on every continent. They died out about 65 million years ago. Today's alligators and crocodiles are related to dinosaurs, but birds are the closest living relatives of dinosaurs!

## extinct

(ik-STINGKT) dinosaurs are extinct and no longer living anywhere in the world

## fossil

(FAH-suhl)—the remains or traces of living things preserved as rock; 200-million-year-old tuatara fossils closely match the skeletons of today's tuataras

# archosaur

(AR-kuh-sor)—a group of reptiles that came before dinosaurs and died out a long time ago; both dinosaurs and crocodiles are related to archosaurs; crocodiles first appeared about 220 million years ago

# tyrannosaurus rex

(ti-RAN-uh-sor-uhs) tyrannosaurus rex was a huge, flesh-eating dinosaur; its closest living relative is the chicken

# stegosaurus

(steg-uh-SOR-uhs)—a dinosaur that fed on plants and had bony plates along its back, a small head, and a long tail with spikes

# triceratops

(try-SER-uh-tops)—a large dinosaur that ate plants and had three horns and a bony collar in the shape of a fan at the back of its head

# Read More

**Bredeson, Carmen.** *Flying Geckos and Other Weird Reptiles.* I Like Weird Animals! Berkeley Heights, N.J.: Enslow Publishers, 2010.

**Kaspar, Anna.** *What's a Reptile?* All about Animals. New York: PowerKids Press, 2012.

**Sirota, Lyn A.** *Chameleons.* Reptiles. Mankato, Minn.: Capstone Press, 2010.

# Internet Sites

FactHound offers a safe, fun way to find Internet sites related to this book. All of the sites on FactHound have been researched by our staff.

Here's all you do:

Visit *www.facthound.com*

Type in this code: 9781429685719

Super-cool stuff!

Check out projects, games and lots more at
**www.capstonekids.com**